Fred & Rose West

The Couple Who Killed Shocking True Serial Killers Stories

Roger Harrington

Copyright © 2017.

All rights reserved. No part of this publication may be reproduced, distributed, or transmitted in any form or by any means, including photocopying, recording, or other electronic or mechanical methods, without the prior written permission of the publisher, except in the case of brief quotations embodied in critical reviews and certain other noncommercial uses permitted by copyright law.

This book is intended for informational and entertainment purposes only. The publisher limits all liability arising from this work to the fullest extent of the law.

Table of Contents

Introduction

Early Lives

Midland Road

25 Cromwell Street

Heather West

Investigation

Trial

Aftermath

Conclusion

Introduction

Some of Britain's most horrific crimes took place in a seemingly normal home. Fred and Rosemary West lived with their nine children at 25 Cromwell Street, in Gloucester, England. The large family was tightknit and was fairly well-liked in the community, but the West household was far from a normal, wholesome home.

Fred and Rose used their house as equal parts brothel and torture dungeon. They put their children, lodgers, and strangers through horrific abuse, torture, and even murder. They did unspeakable things behind closed doors that would eventually give their house the nickname The Gloucester House of Horrors.

The story of Fred and Rose West is proof that we never really know what is going on in other people's lives, and that evil can be happening in the most mundane places, right under our noses.

Early Lives

Frederick Walter Stephen West was born on September 29th, 1941 to Walter Stephen West, and Daisy Hannah Hill, in Much Marcle, Herefordshire. He was their first surviving child, of what would eventually be six children: John, David, Daisy, Douglas, Kathleen, and Gwen. The Wests were an extremely poor farming family who lived in a run-down house without electricity or running water.

Fred alleged that he and his siblings were subject to sexual abuse from both parents. Walter would routinely rape his daughters, and Fred was introduced to sex by his mother at age 12. Fred also claims his father taught him about bestiality at a very young age. The pair would have sexual intercourse with the farm's sheep. Walter West told his son to, "Do what you want, just don't get caught doing it."

Fred's brother, Doug, claims none of Fred's allegations of abuse are true. However, later crimes committed by Fred and his brother John are certainly in keeping with people who have suffered an abusive childhood.

Fred was not a good student. He never fully grasped reading and writing, and was largely illiterate for the rest of his life. Fred was also bullied by his classmates. His mother, Daisy, would often go to the school and yell at teachers for getting Fred in trouble, or at other students for bullying her son. Fred ended up leaving school at 15.

When he was 17, Fred was in a terrible motorcycle accident, and joined the long line of eventual serial killers who sustained a significant head injury in their early life. He was driving his Lambretta down a local street, and collided with a woman going the opposite direction.

Fred broke an arm and a leg, fractured his skull, and was in a coma for eight days. He damaged his frontal cortex; the part of the brain in charge of sexual behavior, judgement, and emotional expression. After this accident, his family noticed he lost control of his emotions, and became even more sexually aggressive than he had been before.

At 19, Fred sustained another head injury. He was at a local youth club, when he began assaulting a young woman. She fought back and ended up pushing Fred off the fire escape. He was unconscious for 24 hours.

In 1961 Fred's attitude continued to decline. He was arrested and fined for theft after stealing a watch strap and a cigarette case.

Fred continued the West family pattern of abuse. He and his brothers followed their father's example, and would also rape his sisters. In 1961, Fred alleges he got his 13 year old sister, Katherine, who they called Kitty, pregnant. His mother reported him to the police. He was arrested, and disowned by his family. It has been speculated that because of his mother's own sexual relationship with her son, Daisy West was jealous of her Fred's relationship with his sister, and only called the police to punish him.

On November 9th, 1961, Fred was charged with assault against a minor for his attacks on his sister. However, when the trial came around, Kitty refused to give evidence against her brother. The case collapsed.

It is not known what happened to the child the two siblings conceived, or indeed whether it ever existed. Fred was known for being a compulsive liar and though there is little doubt he subjected his sister to sexual abuse, he may not have actually conceived with her. Fred also later claimed to several people that he was able to perform crude home abortions. Perhaps he began practicing this skill with his sister.

Fred went to live with an aunt for a short period of time, but eventually was allowed back into the West's house. He began dating an ex-girlfriend, Catherine "Rena" Costello. Rena was a sex worker who was pregnant with another man's child at the time. On November 17th, 1962, she married Fred West, and the couple moved to Lancashire.

Anne Marie, the couple's first biological daughter said of Rena, "My rebellious mother was obsessed with my father and wildly attracted to his strange gypsy looks and bushy brown hair. She wanted him and that was that."

On February 22nd, 1963, Rena's daughter, Charmaine, was born. Charmaine was mixed race and was, therefore, obviously not Fred's child. The couple told Rena's family that she had miscarried the child she was carrying before she married Fred, and that she and Fred had adopted Charmaine.

Soon after Charmaine's birth, Rena became pregnant again. On July 6th, 1964 Anne Marie was born.

The growing family moved to Scotland, where Fred allegedly became acquainted with James Gallogley, an elder in the church, and Alexander Gartshore. Gartshore, who was also the West's neighbor, confessed from prison that Fred had been a part of the paedophile ring the men ran.

In addition to his involvement in the sex ring, Fred may already have started his killing spree by this time. At least four young girls went missing while Fred and Rena were living in Glasgow; one of whom, by the name of Margaret McAvoy, Fred was known to have been acquainted with.

A former neighbor of the Wests said Fred had rented a garden plot adjacent to their houses. He was said to only work there very early in the morning, and he only grew plants on a small patch of it. The neighbor claimed Fred told him the rest of the plot was for "something special".

The garden plots were paved over in the 1970s as part of the M8 motorway expansion. Some believe that road holds secrets of further murders that Fred West took to his grave.

During his time in Scotland, Fred was working as an ice cream van driver. He was popular among the young people in the town, and it has been alleged he found several sexual assault victims through this job.

On November 4th, 1965, Fred West ran over and killed a four year old boy in his ice cream van. It is not known for certain whether this was deliberate. Fred was not prosecuted for this crime, but still decided to flee the area to avoid the scrutiny and hate of the locals. Fred, Rena, Charmaine, and Anne Marie, along with the children's nanny Isa McNeill, and a family friend Anna McFall,

all moved back to England. They lived in a caravan in Lakeside Caravan Park in Bishops Cleeve. Fred continued to be sexually aggressive with all three women, and physically abusive with the children.

Rena and Isa McNeill decided to move back to Scotland to escape Fred's abuse. They left the children with Fred and McFall, occasionally visiting, and attempting to get custody of the children. Fred refused to give them up.

Rena approached Constable Hazel Savage to tell her that Fred was a danger to the children. Savage took an interest in Fred from that point on, and kept the West family on her radar. She would later be instrumental in bringing Fred to justice.

Once settled in the caravan, Fred got a job in a slaughterhouse. It is believed that it was there that Fred West developed his obsession with dismembering corpses, and an interest in necrophilia. Nobody who knew him can remember Fred having such interests before this job.

Anna McFall had become infatuated with Fred during their time together, and the two began a relationship. Anna was consistently insistent that Fred get a legal divorce from Rena so the two could be together. Some suspect Fred got tired of her nagging.

In 1967, when Anna McFall was 8 months pregnant with Fred's child, she disappeared. Fred never reported her missing. Her remains wouldn't be found until 1994, when

Fred told the authorities where they might find her body.

Despite confessing to other killings, Fred never confessed to Anna's murder, and called her his one true love on more than one occasion, even after he married Rosemary. In 1994, Anna was found decapitated and dismembered in Fingerpost Field along with the fetus of her and Fred's unborn child. She was missing her fingers and toes.

A month after McFall's disappearance, Rena moved back in with Fred and her daughters. Fred forced Rena back into sex work in order to support the family. She did not wish to continue that life, and left again shortly after. Charmaine and Anne Marie were temporarily put into foster care.

In January 1968 Fred is strongly suspected to have committed another murder, though he has not been definitively tied to it. Fifteen-year-old Mary Bastholm went missing from a bus stop. Fred certainly had access to her. She was a waitress at Fred's local cafe, The Pop In, and Fred used to do construction work on the building behind the cafe.

On January 6th, 1968, Mary was on her way to Hardwicke to play a game of Monopoly with her boyfriend. She never showed up. A search of the area only turned up a few stray Monopoly pieces at a bridge near where Mary was waiting for the bus.

Years later, Fred confessed to his son, Stephen, that he had killed Mary, though he never admitted the murder to the police. Her body has still never been found.

On November 29th, 1968, 27-year-old Fred West met 15-year-old Rosemary Letts for the first time. He became immediately taken with her. She didn't feel the same way. Rose said of their first meeting, "I was waiting at the bus stop when I noticed this man looking at me. I didn't take to him at all. He was dirty and had work clothes on and looked quite old. This man started talking to me without asking my permission. Within a few minutes he had asked me out. He was like a tramp, a real; mess, and I said 'no'. I thought that was the end of that. Soon after our first meeting I saw him again at the bus stop. He got on the bus with me and started asking me out to pubs."

Fred brought a gift of a silk dress and a fur coat to Rose's workplace to ask her out. Considering the quality of the pieces, it is very likely Fred either stole the items, or got them from a previous murder victim, and gave them to Rose. Rose was impressed with his persistence, and agreed to go out with Fred.

Rosemary Pauline Letts was born on November 29th, 1953 in Devon, to William Andrew "Bill" Letts, and Daisy Gwendoline Fuller. She was the fifth of seven children.

Daisy had been given electro-convulsive shock therapy treatment for depression while she was pregnant with Rose. It is strongly suspected that Rose was born with brain damage because of this. She allegedly exhibited many signs of brain damage in her childhood.

Rose was a slow learner, would occasionally stare into space for extended periods of time, and would often sit alone and rock back and forth. She was also said to have a childlike demeanor, but be fairly sexually aggressive.

Bill ran the Letts household with military precision. There was a set schedule of chores for the children, and he would punish them with beatings if they did not adhere to it. If they did not get out of bed when he told them to, he would dump buckets of cold water over them. Bill would also often fly into fits of rage completely unprovoked. It has since been speculated that he was an undiagnosed, untreated schizophrenic.

Rose was subjected to much the same sexual abuse as Fred West. She was often beaten and raped by her father. Like Fred, Rose continued the cycle of abuse, and began sexually abusing her younger brothers.

As a teenager, Rose began working as a waitress at her sister's boyfriend's diner. She also began sex work in the parking lot of the diner. Rose was allegedly caught in bed with her sister's boyfriend, and was briefly kicked out of her house. When she moved back in just a few months later, rumors began in the neighborhood about a sexual relationship between Bill and Rose.

On her 15th birthday, Rose met Fred at a bus stop. Bill did not like the relationship between Fred and Rose and, as Rose was under the age of consent and Fred was more than 10 years her senior; he tried to get social services involved in their relationship.

At age 16 Rose moved out of her family home to go live with Fred in his trailer. She moved back and forth from the two residences, while Fred spent various stints in jail for theft during the first few months of their relationship.

Fred's children, Charmaine and Anne Marie, also moved between the trailer and foster care homes. While Fred was in jail, Rose was in charge of their care. She treated Fred's children horribly, beating them regularly. Anne Marie said, "It was obvious from the start that Rose had a hell of a temper, and was not able to control it".

Charmaine got the worst of Rose's abuse. Anne Marie said later stated that Charmaine, "would go out of her way to antagonize and aggravate our volatile stepmother", and that she "never missed a chance to remind rose about our real mother". It aggravated Rose even more that Charmaine would never cry when she was beaten.

Rose was kicked out of her family home for good when Bill found out she was pregnant. The family moved into a bigger home, a two-story house on Midland Road in Gloucester. On October 17th, 1970, Fred and Rose's first daughter, Heather, was born. Fred went back to jail for another theft charge on December 4th, 1970.

Midland Road

While he was in jail Rose's abuse of Fred's children got worse. In 1971 Rose wrote a suspicious note to Fred that read, "Darling, about Char. I think she liked to be handled rough. But darling, why do I have to be the one to do it. I would keep her for her own sake if it wasn't for the rest of the children. You can see Char coming out [i]n Anna now and I hate it."

In March of 1971 Charmaine was taken to the hospital with a puncture wound through her ankle. Doctors noted that the wound could have been from a knife, but they did not follow up on the potential abuse happening in the home, nor did they inform the police.

The family visited Fred in prison on June 17th, 1971. A few days later Charmaine went missing. Rose told Anne Marie that their mother, Rena, had come in the middle of the night to collect Charmaine.

Rose had actually murdered the young girl, and buried her in a coal pit in the cellar. Fred got out of jail in late July 1971, and helped Rose move the body to a new burial site in the garden. When the landlady of their Midland Road home asked Fred to build an extension on the home, he built the new kitchen over Charmaine's grave.

When her remains were found years later they exhibited telltale signs of Fred having been involved in her burial. Like Anna McFall before her, Charmaine's body was missing the kneecaps, and some fingers and toes. Fred kept these bones as trophies of his kills. Many of his later victims would also be found missing those bones. The various bones have never been found.

In August of 1971, Rena did come back to England to collect her children. She asked Fred's father where she could find him. Fred and Rena went to a local pub where Fred plied his wife with alcohol. He then molested her and strangled her to death in the back of his car. Rena was decapitated, dismembered, and buried in Letterbox Field. Her remains were not found until Fred's confession over twenty years later.

On January 29th, 1972, Fred and Rose got married. Rose said of their wedding, "I had to beg [Fred] to take off his overalls. His brother John witnessed the marriage, and another friend of Fred's who had so many aliases he had to scribble out the first name he wrote on the certificate."

Fred signified himself as a bachelor on the marriage certificate, which Rose did not object to. Some have pointed to this as evidence that Rose knew Fred's first wife, Rena, was already dead.

Fred's brother John not only helped the two get married; he also allegedly began aiding the couple in their horrific crimes. John would often have sex with Rose, and rape Anna Marie and a younger West child. He also used his job to help Fred and Rose cover up their murders. John was a garbage man, and would allegedly allow the couple to dispose of body parts, or victims' possessions in his truck, to avoid the suspicions of the neighbors, and the local sanitary workers.

25 Cromwell Street

Rose was pregnant with the couple's second child when they got married. The growing West family decided they needed more room to live. Fred, Rose, Anne Marie, and Heather, moved to 25 Cromwell Street, in Gloucester. Charmaine's absence was not yet conspicuous. On June 1st of the same year, Rose gave birth to their second biological daughter, Mae.

Fred converted the large house into several rental apartments and bedsits. There could have been up to 30 people living there at any given time. The house was not a good neighborhood. Shaun Boyle, the boyfriend of a former lodger said 25 Cromwell was "well known as a place where drifters and dropouts and teenagers who had been kicked out of home could look for bedsits. You'd never question it if someone moved on."

Rose began doing sex work out of one of the rooms under the name Mandy, the same pseudonym Rena used. Fred installed peep holes into the room where she worked so he could watch his wife sleep with other men. Bill Letts, Rose's father, would often come to the makeshift brothel and have sex with his own daughter.

In October of 1972, the Wests found a woman hitchhiking. Seventeen year old Caroline Owens took a ride from the Wests, and agreed to be their live-in nanny. Caroline was immediately uncomfortable in the house. Fred and Rose would constantly ask her about her sex life, and insist she and her boyfriend use their bed for sex. Fred also claimed he could perform abortions and promised to help her if she ever "got into trouble."

Caroline quit the nanny job and left the house. A few weeks later she was picked up by the Wests again while hitchhiking.

Caroline was bound in the van, and Rose began to assault her before they even made it back to the house. She said "[Fred] stopped the car, turned around in the seat and punched me until I was knocked out. I was tied up and my mouth was taped. They sneaked me into the house, and it was 12 hours of sexual assault. Mostly by Rose." She said her experience with Rose was much more disturbing than her experience with Fred. She felt "utterly degraded".

Before Caroline got out of Cromwell Road, Fred threatened her that he would "bury [her] under the paving stones of Gloucester", and implied that there were "hundreds of girls" already there. She was only able to escape after she agreed to be the children's nanny again.

She, Rose, and two of the girls took a trip to the laundromat. Rose ran into a tenant of 25 Cromwell and, while she was distracted by conversation, Caroline ran.

Caroline filed charges against Fred and Rose but did not push a rape charge. She didn't want everyone knowing her personal business, and her step-father was worried about the neighbors gossiping about their family. Fred and Rose were found guilty of the lesser charge of indecent assault. They were both charged the measly sum of £50.

Caroline believed for years that she was the reason Fred and Rose began killing their victims, and blamed her for the subsequent deaths of the other women. She said, "After it came out, I felt terribly emotional and guilty. I thought I'd been selfish because my first thought was to protect myself, even though the Wests' behavior had been suspicious - I didn't want people to probe into my life. If I had really persisted, the police would at least have been watching Fred. And, on the flip side, if I hadn't said anything at all, would the women still have been alive? Because I caused a fuss Fred and Rose no longer trusted the women they abused, and so eradicated their fears by killing them."

Of course Caroline was not to blame for any of the crimes the ghoulish pair would later commit. Both Wests had already killed separately, and nothing would stop them from doing it again, together. Stephen West, the pair's first son, blames a shoddy system for his parents' further crimes. He said, "All they got was a fine. It was like a green light. You know, go for it."

Just a few weeks after the trial for Caroline's abuse, the couple began a horrific string of murders that would eventually give 25

Cromwell Street the nickname The House of Horrors.

Nineteen year old Lynda Gough was the first victim the Wests killed together. Lynda was a seamstress who was having multiple affairs with lodgers at 25 Cromwell Street, and who the pair asked to be the children's nanny. As a result she had become acquainted with Fred and Rose. The three ended up sharing a bed together on several occasions. On April 19th, 1973 she left home abruptly and did not return.

Her mother began asking around the neighborhood for clues as to where her daughter may have gone. Her search led her to the Cromwell Street house. She knocked on the door and asked Rose where her daughter was. Rose made a show of attempting to remember Lynda, and then told Mrs. Gough the girl had briefly stayed with them, but had moved to Weston-super-Mare. Mrs. Gough noticed Rose was wearing items of Lynda's clothing, including her slippers, and that there were more of her belongings hanging on the washing line.

Lynda had not moved away. Rose was wearing a dead girl's clothes. Fred and Rose had killed Lynda, dismembered her body, and buried her in the floor beneath their bathroom. When her body was found over 20 years later it appeared her head had been wrapped in a tape mask fitted with breathing tubes placed in her nostrils to briefly keep her alive while they tortured her.

Investigators also found string and rope buried with her body. Fred later admitted he liked to string his victims up from the beams on the cellar ceiling.

Lynda most likely died of suffocation or strangulation. Her body was missing kneecaps and some fingers, a trademark of Fred West.

The Wests next victim was 15-year-old Carol Ann Cooper. She was living in Pine's Children's Home in Worcester. On November 10th, 1973, Carol was waiting at a bus stop, heading home after seeing a movie with her boyfriend. She was most likely pushed into Fred's van and bound there before being smuggled into the house, similar to the abduction of Caroline Roberts.

She was also hung from the cellar ceiling, assaulted, and murdered. She was decapitated, her body was dismembered, and she buried under the cellar floor.

Just one month after Carol Ann Cooper, the Wests targeted Lucy Partington. Lucy was a 21-year-old Exeter University student who was visiting home for Christmas vacation. She left a friend's house at 10:15 on December 27th, 1973, and was never seen by her friends or family again.

Lucy was also decapitated and buried under the floor of the cellar. It is believed that the Wests kept her alive for several days before killing her. Lucy's body was found buried with the knife that was used to dismember her.

On January 3rd, 1974, Fred admitted himself to the hospital with a serious laceration on his right hand that required several stitches. The wound was consistent with the size, shape, and depth of a wound one might get if injured with the knife found with Lucy's body. Investigators believe Fred sustained the injury while dismembering Lucy.

In April 1974 the couple picked up Therese Siegenthaler, a Swiss student who was studying sociology at Greenwich Community College, and was attempting to hitchhike across England. She, too, ended up buried in the cellar. Fred and Rose mistook her Swiss accent for a Dutch one, and would refer to her as Tulip.

Their next killing also took place that year. Fifteen year old Shirley Hubbard went missing in November of 1974. She was a foster child who was attending a work experience program. Shirley was abducted at a bus stop while on the way home from a date with her boyfriend. Her body was found in the cellar with a tape mask and a breathing tube similar to that of Lynda Gough's.

Brian Leveson, the lawyer for the prosecution, explained the purpose of the tape masks during the West's trial, "The breathing tube or tubes demonstrate that Shirley must have been alive when the mask was applied. Its purpose can only have been to keep her wholly under control, unable to see, unable to cry out, just able to breathe."

They wanted utter control of the victim while they tortured and abused her.

In April of 1975 Fred and Rose killed the last woman who would be buried in the cellar. Eighteen-year-old Juanita Mott was a former lodger at 25 Cromwell, who then moved out to live with friends. While hitchhiking along B4215 Juanita was picked up by the Wests and taken back to Cromwell Road. She was also decapitated and dismembered before being buried under the floor in the cellar.

After Fred buried Juanita the killer couple ran out of room in the cellar to hide the bodies of their victims. Fred poured concrete over the graves, and made the torture chamber into another room in the house, where his oldest daughters would sleep.

There are no known murders between Juanita in April 1975 and their next murder in 1978, but the couple hadn't reformed in those few years. During the trial years later an anonymous woman, simply known as Miss A, came forward saying she escaped Fred and Rose at the height of their killing spree.

In 1977, when Miss A was 15 years old, she ran away from an area children's home, and ended up at Cromwell. She befriended the Wests and, when she decided to run away again, she went to them. She said she was taken to a room where she was confronted with two other girls, who were both, naked. Rose stripped and assaulted her, and Fred raped her.

Oddly, Fred and Rose let Miss a go. Considering their compulsion for torture and murder, as well as all they had to lose by having the police investigate them, it seems strange that they would let a potential murder victim--and potential informant--go free.

During the trial, Leveson said the Wests, "obviously made an assessment that this girl would not go to the police." Still, it was a dangerous move that was probably born of their growing arrogance.

Some suggest that the Wests may have found young girls who were allowing them to act out their sexually fantasies with them, so the kidnappings and rapes slowed down.

Others think the couple was still killing, and just buried them somewhere other than 25 Cromwell. Author Geoffrey Wansell, writer of the in depth biography of the Wests, An Evil Love: The Life of Frederick West, said, "Serial killers don't stop until they are caught. There cannot be much doubt that Fred and Rosemary carried on killing after they had buried all those remains in Cromwell Street. Almost certainly they found other places to dispose of victims".

Wansell has also claimed, "I would not be surprised if there were more than 90."

In April 1977 an 18-year-old woman named Shirley Robinson came to stay at 25 Cromwell. She began an affair with Fred and became pregnant by him. Rose was also pregnant by a client at the time. Rose used to brag to the neighbors that Shirley was pregnant with her husband's child.

Investigators believe that the novelty of this affair grew tired for Rose, and she began to be threatened by Shirley's relationship with Fred. Fred, too, was allegedly tired of Shirley. He told his brother-in-law, Jim-Tyler, "She wants to get between me and Rose. She wants Rose out so she can take over and take her place. I'm not having that, she's got to fucking go."

When she was 8 months pregnant, Shirley was murdered, dismembered and decapitated. Unlike the other women, she was buried in the garden at 25 Cromwell.

After her death, Rose attempted to claim a maternity benefit from Social Services in Shirley's name.

In August 1979 the Wests invited 16-year-old Alison Chambers to be their live-in nanny. She was a runaway from a local children's home, who was actually still in touch with her family, who, presumably simply didn't have the means to take care of her. Alison was the second victim to be buried in a garden grave.

In order to make it seem like Alison had simply moved away, Fred and Rose posted a letter to Alison's mother that she had written before they murdered her. They sent it from a Northamptonshire postbox that was approximately a 2 hour drive from Gloucester.

Between 1974 and 1980 Rose had had six more children, two of whom were conceived with one of her Jamaican clients. The West family now consisted of Fred, Rose, Anne Marie, Mae, Heather, Stephen, Tara, Rosemary, Lucyanna, Louise, and Barry.

The West siblings were being constantly terrorized by their parents. Rose's brother, Graham Letts said, "Whenever we (he and his wife) walked into the house there was never any noise. Even with nine or ten children around, you could hear a pin drop...It reminded me in some ways of our mom. Rosie was every bit as strict, and seemed to be using the same tactics: 'If you don't do as I say, you'll regret it.'"

Heather West

Just as Rose's brother suspected, Rose and her husband were indeed severely abusing their children. They were all savagely beaten for reasons Rosemary would fabricate. Stephen recalls an incident where his mother called him home from school to tie him up and beat him for something his sister had actually done.

If the children weren't being abused they were being ignored. They were completely in charge of their own upbringing, having to do all their own cooking and cleaning from the time they were seven years old.

Anne Marie was not only physically abused. Fred would sexually abuse her daily from the time she was ten. She said, "I was told I should be grateful and that I was lucky I had such caring parents who thought of me...My father's abuse continued without a break until I ran away from home at fifteen."

At fifteen Anne Marie discovered she was pregnant by her father. The pregnancy ended up being ectopic, wherein the embryo attaches to the fallopian tube wall, instead of the uterus, and Anne Marie had an abortion.

She moved in with her boyfriend, Christopher Davis. The young couple was running low on funds, and was forced to move into the West home for a brief period. Christopher noticed how tense the house made Anne Marie, and how strangely disconnected from reality Heather acted. The two girls confided in him everything that their parents had done to them.

Christopher said he would confront the Wests on behalf of the girls, but Anne Marie begged him not to saying, "For Christ's sake doesn't, because they'll kill us both."

Anne Marie and Christopher moved out again and started a family. Heather asked to live with them but, as she was not yet 16--the age she would be allowed to legally leave home--Anne Marie knew Fred and Rose would make sure Heather ended up back at 25 Cromwell with them.

When Anne Marie left home, Fred turned his attentions to Mae and Heather. He refused to let them lock the door while they showered, and would come into their bathroom to fondle them while they were naked. The girls began standing guard for each other while the other one showered, in an attempt to avoid their father's abuse.

Fred also installed a peep hole in their bedroom, and would watch them change. They had no privacy, and no refuge from the constant abuse. Heather used to talk about running away and living a peaceful life in the Forest of Dean.

Heather took the abuse the worst. Mae said, "She was so miserable, but she never talked about it. She just became a loner and a bit of a recluse." She would alternate between being totally despondent, and being aggressive. She would rarely even socialize with her own siblings. When the family would visit Anne Marie, Heather would stand alone at the edge of the yard, and not speak to anyone.

She was the same at school. Although she was a good student, some staff recognized that Heather experienced severe mood swings. One of her teachers described her as, "Jekyll and Hyde. One minute nice as pie and the next very aggressive."

Heather's teachers also noticed that she refused to change or shower after physical activity. After she was forced to shower, her friend Denise Harrison noticed that Heather was covered in bruises and sores.

Heather confided in Denise that she was being abused by her parents. Rumors about the West household began swirling. Heather admitted most of the rumors were true. One of her classmates told their parents, who were friends of the Wests. They told Fred that Heather had been gossiping about their family.

Anne Marie said, "Fred and Rose were furious that Heather had been discussing their business outside the family, and she suffered a tremendous beating." Fred also began escorting Heather to and from school, to further isolate her from the outside world.

Denise told her parents about what Heather told her, but they also knew the Wests and didn't believe they were capable of such horrors. If someone had followed up and tried to protect Heather, maybe what happened next could have been prevented.

Anne Marie wrote, "I remember the last time I saw Heather; I even recall what she was wearing. She had on a baggy white T-shirt and leggings. Her dark brown hair was very long and worn loose. I made a note of it in my diary which later helped the police pinpoint exactly when she went missing. The date was 17 June, 1987--my elder daughter Michelle's 3rd birthday."

The next day Heather received a rejection from a job she had applied to. She had finished school earlier that year and had begun applying to cleaning jobs at hotels in holiday towns. A job she had gotten in

Torque had fallen through at the last minute. Her dream of getting away from her parents had been crushed. Mae said she "cried all the way through the night."

On June 19th, Mae and Stephen saw Heather sitting sullenly on the couch before they left for school. By the time they got home Heather had disappeared. Fred told them she had actually gone to Torque to see if she could get the job.

Fred had actually strangled his daughter to death, dismembered and decapitated her, and placed her body parts in garbage bins to await a convenient time to bury her.

Anne Marie said, "Dad said it was early morning. He strangled her in the hallway.

He hot one of the black bins from the house, cut her legs and arms off, put her in the dustbin, put the lid on, and put her in the cupboard under the basement stairs. Then he said, we went to bed at 9pm, and he buried her in the garden."

Fred collected some of Heather's clothes and belongings in garbage bags, and put them in the trash cans of a neighborhood veterinary clinic. They would be taken away in the garbage collection, and it would look as though Heather had packed up and left. Stephen noticed his sister didn't take a book she had recently won that was her most prized possession.

Stephen says Fred made him dig his sister's grave under the presence that he was going to build a fish pond in their garden. "He told me 'I want a hole there, about four feet deep and six across, and I want you to lay blue plastic in the hole and leave it'".

A few days later the hole was filled in, and no fish pond was built. Fred had paved over the area with pink and yellow patio stones, and had built a barbeque pit adjacent to it. The family would have cookouts on Heather's grave.

In the following years, Fred and Rose told many stories of where Heather had gone. They said she had run away with a lesbian lover, and said she was probably working as a prostitute or drug dealer under an assumed name. When the other children grew concerned they hadn't heard from her,

Fred said they shouldn't involve the police, as Heather was wanted for credit card fraud, and she would get in trouble if they found her.

The Wests then began receiving phone calls from "Heather". The phone would ring and either Fred or Rose would pick it up, and have a conversation in front of the children with whoever was on the other end of the line. Of course the kids were never allowed to speak to whoever was pretending to be their sister. Sometimes Rose would even get into an argument with the fake Heather. Fred would also claim to have seen her in various places.

Between performances of pretending Heather was alive, Fred would threaten his other children that they'd "end up under the patio like Heather"

Rosemary allegedly changed significantly after Heather disappeared. Photos of Heather were removed from the home, the children were forbidden to speak of her, and Rose would spend hours alone sobbing.

Mae said her mother never hit her again after that point.

Investigation

In May 1992 Fred began sexually abusing one of his younger daughters, allegedly recording one of the rapes. The West daughter told a friend about what had happened to her.

In August 1992 the friend asked a police officer what to do if someone was being abused by their family. The officer alerted Social Services to the rumors about the West house. Authorities obtained a warrant to search 25 Cromwell Street for evidence of child pornography and child abuse.

On August 6th, 1992 Fred West was arrested and charged with rape and sodomy. Rose was arrested for child cruelty, and being an accomplice to her husband's sexual abuse. The five youngest children were taken from 25 Cromwell and put in care at Jordan's Brook Community Home.

They were extensively interviewed and given physical examinations. Evidence of physical and sexual abuse was clearly present. The children all explained the abuse they had suffered at the hands of their parents. The girls described how Fred would sexually abuse them, and Rose would tell them they were "asking for it" and that they deserved it.

Anne Marie heard her father had been arrested for abuse, but was maintaining his innocence. On August 7th, 1992 Anne Marie made an extensive statement to Constable

Savage about the abuse she suffered in the West house. She said, "I went through hell making that statement to Hazel. It brought back horrors I thought I had blocked out forever. It shook me to the core and left me traumatized."

She also told Constable Savage that she had been looking for her mother, Rena, and her half-sister, Charmaine, for years and had not been able to locate them.

On June 7th, 1993 the Wests were brought before Judge Gabriel Hutton. Fred was charged with three counts of rape and sodomy; Rose faced charges for "causing or encouraging the commission of unlawful sexual intercourse with a girl under the age of 16", and "cruelty to a child."

On the day of the trial the children refused to testify against their parents. The case against them collapsed, and Fred was allowed to return to live at 25 Cromwell.

Anne Marie also retracted the statement she made to the police. This may have been because of a phone call from her mother where she vaguely threatened her. Rose told Anne Marie, "If you think anything of me or your dad you'll keep your mouth shut." She feared what might happen if she angered Rose. Anne Marie also saw the distress the ordeal was causing her sister, and decided not to push it. She did, however, continue to ask for help in finding Rena and Charmaine.

Constable Savage, knowing Fred's dark past, continued to believe Anne Marie's statement was true. She would spend the next year searching for signs of Heather. British authorities decided to involve Interpol to see whether Heather had fled the country. No evidence of her existence was found.

The rest of the West children were still in foster care. Social workers began hearing them speak of a threat their father would frequently use against them when they were misbehaving. He told them they would "end up under the patio like Heather" if they didn't cooperate.

The police took the West children's statements regarding the patio at Cromwell, and used them to obtain a warrant to dig up the garden at the West family home. On

February 23rd, 1994, authorities began work excavating the Wests garden.

Rose called Fred at work and told him they were digging up the garden. Fred went to Gloucester Police Station to voluntarily give a statement; only his statement was completely false. He told Detective Constable Hazel Savage that he had seen Heather recently, in Birmingham.

He also said that she had most likely changed her name and become a prostitute, or was working with a drug cartel in Bahrain. Authorities did not yet have any reason to detain Fred, so he was allowed to return home.

Rose was interviewed separately at her home, but also maintained that she did not know where Heather was.

On February 25th, 1994, Detective Constables Savage and Law came to 25 Cromwell in order to collect information on the Wests family members, so that they could interview the extended family about Heather's disappearance.

Fred asked the detectives if he could be taken to the police station. In the car he confessed to Constable Savage that he had actually killed his daughter.

Fred said he choked Heather to death by accident after an argument about her moving out of the house. He told Savage, "I lunged at her…and grabbed her throat…and I held for a minute. How long I held her for I don't know, I can't remember…I can just remember lunging for her throat and the next minute she's gone blue. I looked at her and, I mean, I was shaking from head to foot, I mean, what the heck had gone wrong?"

Fred said his wife knew nothing of Heather's murder, but she was arrested on suspicion of murder anyway.

After taking his statement the detectives took Fred back to 25 Cromwell to point out where Heather's grave was.

Just one day after making a full confession, Fred retracted his statement about Heather's murder. He said, "Heather is not in the garden. Heather's alive and well...I have no idea what her name is, because I won't let her tell me. She contacts me when she's in this country...They can dig there for evermore. Nobody or nothing's under my patio."

Since obtaining the search warrant on February 24th, fifteen police officers had been working tirelessly in the rain to excavate the West's yard. On February 26th, after Fred had retracted his statement about Heather being buried in the garden, the search team found a femur belonging to an unknown person, and Heather West's skeleton. Heather had been dismembered and decapitated. She, like Fred's other victims, was missing a kneecap, and several finger and toe bones.

Fred re-confessed to Heather's murder. He was questioned about the other femur found in the garden, and was fairly straightforward with investigators. He said it probably belonged to Shirley Robinson, "the girl who caused the problem."

Fred then said Shirley's friend was buried somewhere in the garden, too. He admitted to strangling and killing Alison Chambers, who he could not identify by name. Rose was arrested on suspicion of the murder of Shirley Robinson, and an unknown female.

On February 27th, 1994 Fred was formally charged with Heather West's murder. He once again claimed that his wife knew nothing of his murders, and she was let out on bail.

Fred was assigned an appropriate adult, Janet Leach. An appropriate adult usually assists minors who have been brought in for questioning in understanding the legal proceedings. Due to Fred's illiteracy, he was also eligible for this service. Janet was a 38-year-old, divorced mother of five, who was working toward being a social worker.

Fred became quite taken with Janet. She was said to closely resemble Anna McFall, and some believed Fred was actually in love with her. Janet spent 400 hours with Fred over the short period she was assigned to his case.

Janet said she became a confidant of Fred's; he would only speak to the police when she was in the room, and he began to confess crimes to her that he would not admit to the police. He referred to her as his "only friend".

She said Fred was extremely blasé about his crimes. She said, "He showed no emotion. No pity. No remorse. We might have been discussing the weather."

Janet's confidentiality agreement prevented her from telling the police the horrific things Fred admitted to her when they were out of the room. The knowledge of his crimes weighed on Janet. She threatened to quit her position if Fred did not confess to the police.

On February 28th the remains of Shirley Robinson and her unborn child, and Alison Chambers were pulled from the ground at 25 Cromwell Road. The media had gotten a hold of the story, and people began coming forward asking if their missing loved ones had been found in the garden. Fred was asked about Lynda Gough after her family said she had been last seen around 25 Cromwell.

On March 4th, 1994 Fred made a full, handwritten confession stating "I, Frederick West, authorize my solicitor, Howard Ogden, to advise Superintendent Bennett that I wish to admit to a further (approx.) nine killings, expressly Charmaine, Rena, Lynda Gough, and others to be identified"

Fred confessed that there were five more bodies buried under the floor in the cellar, one more in the main floor bathroom, one under the kitchen at the Midland Road home, one in Fingerpost Field, and one in Letterbox Field.

He maintained Rose knew nothing of the murders. He also claimed that he never deliberately tortured or murdered anyone, saying, "Yeah, see, you've got the killing all wrong, no, nobody went through hell, enjoyment turned to disaster, well most of it anyway."

The condition of the bodies and testimony from surviving victims made it clear that a victim's time with the Wests was far from consensual, and the murders were not simply sadistic sex acts that accidently went too far.

Fred allegedly admitted to Stephen that his victims were missing fingers, toes, and kneecaps because he would remove them as a form of torture while the victim was still alive.

Fred was again taken back to Cromwell to point out where the other graves were. On March 5th, Therese Siegenthaler and Shirley Hubbard were found, and Fred was taken to Letterbox Field to point out Rena's burial place. Lucy Partington and Juanita Mott were found on the 6th.

On the 7th Lynda Gough was found, and Fred was taken to Fingerpost Field to point out Anna McFall's grave. Fred never admitted to killing Anna, and always claimed she was the love of his life. He had no explanation, though, for how he knew she was dead, or how he knew where she was buried.

Carol Ann Cooper was found on March 8th. Police obtained a search warrant for 25 Midland Road, and Charmaine's remains were found there on May 4th.

Trial

On June 30th, 1994, Fred and Rosemary West were brought to court to be jointly charged for the murders of the women found in their home. Rose was to be sentenced for nine of the murders, and Fred was to face sentencing for eleven.

Fred attempted to make contact with his wife, reaching out to touch her and speak in her ear. Rose publicly rebuffed him, and recoiled at his touch. This angered and embarrassed Fred, who then retracted his statements that Rose knew nothing of the murders.

Anna McFall's body had been found in Fingerpost Field on June 7th, but she had not been positively identified until after the June 30th hearing. Fred was charged with the murder of Anna McFall on July 3rd, 1994.

A little after noon, on January 1st, 1995, while awaiting trial and sentencing for all 12 known murders, Fred West committed suicide by hanging in his cell at Winson Green Prison, Birmingham. He had allegedly created a suicide kit consisting of bed sheets, razor blades, and a cotton reel, that was found six days after he entered the prison. It was not confiscated. Seven months later Fred used it to take his own life.

Fred's suicide note read:

"To Rose West, Steve and Mae,

Well Rose it's your birthday on 29 November 1994 and you will be 41 and still beautiful and still lovely and I love you. We will always be in love. The most wonderful thing in my life was when I met you. Our love is special to us. So, love, keep your promises to me. You know what they are. Where we are put together for ever and ever is up to you. We loved Heather, both of us. I would love Charmaine to be with Heather and Rena. You will always be Mrs. West, all over the world. That is important to me and to you. I haven't got you a present, but all I have is my life. I will give it to you, my darling. When you are ready, come to me. I will be waiting for you."

At the bottom of his note he had drawn a headstone with the words "In loving memory. Fred West. Rose West. Rest in peace where no shadow falls. In perfect peace he waits for Rose, his wife" written on it.

Rose said of her husband's suicide "I am so relieved. He was evil. He should have died long ago."

Even after the questioning had finished, Janet Leach continued to visit and write to Fred. She was allegedly devastated at the loss of Fred. Her son, Paul, said she "fell under West's spell" and she was deeply affected by his suicide. It does seem as though the two shared a special bond.

Rose had gone through six different appropriate adults during her questionings.

They couldn't stand to listen to the details of what went on at 25 Cromwell. Janet, though, was present for almost every questioning, additional confession, and continued to visit Fred after her role as appropriate adult had finished.

Janet claims she was not upset at his loss, but frustrated and upset that he died with more secrets. She said Fred had told her there were twenty more bodies to be found. Janet said, "I was desperate. I couldn't sleep at night. I kept having nightmares about those poor girls in the cellar. But I felt I had to keep talking to Fred. Otherwise, how would their families know what had happened to them?"

Fred was cremated on March 29th, 1995. A service was held which only Tara, Stephen, and Mae attended. Other families having funerals that day were outraged that their loved one had to share a funeral date and place with Fred West.

The service only lasted five minutes. It was an unsentimental, borderline hostile affair where Fred was not remembered fondly. Reverend Smith told the West children present that they should, "remember everyone else who has also suffered because of these tragic events."

Fred West's ashes were scattered at the Welsh seaside resort he named his son after, Barry Island; a place he visited as a child, and as a father with his own children.

After Fred recanted his statement that Rose didn't know anything of the killings, Rose was also charged with Charmaine's murder, bringing her count up to ten.

Rose's trial began on October 3rd, 1995. During the seven weeks of evidence, the jury heard from former tenants of 25 Cromwell Road, Anne Marie West, Caroline Owens, Miss A--the anonymous woman who Fred and Rose assaulted in 1977--, and Rose's own family members.

Rose herself made the choice to testify in her own trial, against the advice of her counsel. She opened her statements by attempting to set herself up as another one of Fred's victims. She said, "He had promised me the world, promised me everything and because

I was so young I fell for his lies but because I was so young I did not realize they were lies at the time. He promised to love me and care for me and I fell for it."

Rose attempted to claim Fred did not let her in the cellar where several of the murders took place, and where most of the bodies were found. She said he would lock the door and do his business in secret. Those who survived Rose's abuse know this is far from the truth. Even Fred alluded to Rose being the more sexually aggressive one of the pair.

Detective Superintendent John Bennett, the Senior Investigating Officer on the case said, "The whole case was about Rosemary being sexually insatiable. There were huge quantities of pornographic material and sex objects in the house. I firmly believe that Rose murdered the girls and Fred disposed of the bodies."

Rose did herself no favors on the stand. She laughed and joked during her testimony, and told blatant lies. After being shown photographs of her victims she said she didn't remember six of the ten women she was being charged with murdering.

Of the assault on Caroline Owens, which was known to be an aggressive assault largely perpetrated by Rose, she said, "As soon as she put up resistance, as soon as I realized that she was against this, that she did not agree with it in any way I stopped. All I can remember is being very frightened. Fred was a threat at this moment in time. I was pleading with Fred all the time for it to stop. I didn't want to get involved in anything like this. I didn't want Caroline to get hurt. It was just a mess."

Rose only became somewhat emotional when Heather was brought up. However, many believe her tears were just an act.

Janet Leach, Fred's appropriate adult, testified that she had become a confidant of Fred's and that he had told her Rose "played a major part" in all the murders. She said Fred had told her the murders were largely "Rose's mistakes" where an act of sexual sadism went too far, and the victim ended up dead.

Janet testified that Fred had confided in her about a pact between him and Rose where he would take full responsibility for all the murders.

Janet also lied under oath about having sold her story to the press. She had actually sold her account of her friendship with Fred to the Daily Mirror for £100,000.

Janet had been experiencing severe health problems because of her involvement with Fred West, and her exclusive knowledge of many of his crimes. While she was testifying on the stand at Rose's trial, Janet collapsed. She had had a stroke.

The trial was halted for six days while Janet recovered. When she returned to the stand she confessed she had lied about selling her story.

The trial ended on November 16th, 1995. On November 21st, the jury found Rose guilty of the murder of Charmaine West, Heather West, and Shirley Robinson. The next day, the jury found Rose guilty of the murders of the remaining seven women: Lynda Gough, Carol Ann Cooper, Lucy Partington, Therese Siegenthaler, Shirley Hubbard, Juanita Mott, and Alison Chambers.

The judge sentenced Rose to life in prison with the recommendation that she never be let out. He called her crimes "appalling and depraved".

A life sentence in England at the time did not actually mean a person would spend the remainder of their life in prison. It meant they would serve a minimum of 15 years before parole would be entertained. The Lord Chief Justice declared Rosemary should spend at least 25 years in prison.

Rose continued to protest her innocence. Barry West has said, "My mum continually lies about her involvement in the hopes that one day she'll be free, but she knows every detail of what took place."

On July 1997, Home Secretary Jack Straw gave Rose a life tariff, ensuring she would never get out of prison. Rose allegedly became close friends with Myra Hindley, another woman who had committed serial murders with her partner, and one of the only other women in UK history to be serving a whole life tariff.

Aftermath

25 Cromwell Street

On October 7th, 1996, Gloucester City Council began demolition of the House of Horrors at 25 Cromwell Street. The council had bought the house and the adjoining vacant lot for £40,000. The money from the sale went to the solicitor who was dealing with Fred West's estate. It was used to set up a trust for the five youngest West children.

Dismantling the house took 15 days. It was destroyed completely to avoid souvenir seekers getting a piece of the horrific history. The bricks were removed one-by-one, crushed, mixed with other materials, and used in undisclosed projects. The wood beams were all burned. The rivets and other metal were all melted. The foundations were filled in and capped with two feet of concrete.

A concrete pathway is all that exists on the lot now.

The West children

The five youngest West children were still in care when their father committed suicide and their mother went to prison for life. Tara, Barry, and Louise still live in Gloucester. Lucyanna and Rosemary Jr moved to the south of England

Anne Marie attempted suicide several times during her life. In 1999 she threw herself from a Gloucester bridge into the water below, and was carried quite a distance down river. She was pulled from the water, barely alive, by fire fighters.

She made a heartbreaking statement about her attempts to end her life, "People say I am lucky to have survived, but I wish I had died. I can still taste the fear. Still feel the pain."

As part of her healing process Anne Marie wrote a book about her childhood called Out of the Shadows: Fred West's Daughter Tells Her Harrowing Story of Survival.

Her partner Phil Davies has said, "Life has been a nightmare for Anne Marie, because she keeps reliving the trauma. What she's been through is unimaginably hard for anyone to cope with, but I'm so proud of her. It's a heavy burden, but she's just trying to lead an ordinary life now. With me and the kids supporting her, I think she can see a light at the end of the tunnel."

At Anne Marie's request, her mother, Rena, and her half-sister, Charmaine, were buried in the same coffin.

Stephen West also attempted suicide in January 2002, by hanging. Like his sister, he survived.

In December 2004, Stephen went to prison for 9 months for inappropriate sexual relations with a fourteen year old girl.

Stephen lamented "There's a bit of my dad in me."

At his trial Stephen's barrister, Stephen Mooney, said, "He had one of the most traumatic and distressing childhoods one can imagine, and what happened affected his emotional development. Anyone who had suffered like him had a tendency to remain emotionally less well-developed for his age."

Stephen co-wrote a book with his sister, Mae, about their experiences called Inside 25 Cromwell Street: The Terrifying True Story of a Life with Fred and Rose West.

Mae attempted to hide her identity. She changed her last name, and had plastic surgery to remove a distinctive mole from her face. She dropped off the radar and didn't speak out for 17 years, until 2011 when she said she realized, "Not talking doesn't make it go away". Mae says she has forgiven her parents.

Stephen, Tara, and Mae had a proper funeral for Heather on December 19th, 1995. It was held at St. Michael's parish church at Tintern, near the Forest of Dean where Heather always dreamed of running away to live. Rose wanted to be allowed to attend, but was not granted permission to leave prison for the service.

The other West

Fred's brother, John hanged himself in his garage on November 28th, 1996. During police questioning Fred said John aided him and his wife in disposing of evidence of their murders. At the time of his death he was awaiting a decision from a trial where he faced rape charges. Anne Marie reported that her uncle raped her over 300 times while she lived at 25 Cromwell Street. He would also go to the house to have sex with Rosemary.

There is no solid evidence linking John to his brother's murders but, considering his rape charges, and close relationship with his brother, it is certainly possible that those rumors are true.

Other notable people

Caroline Owens wrote two books on her experiences with the Wests: The Lost Girl: How I Triumphed Over Life at the Mercy of Fred and Rose West, and The One That Got Away: My Life Living With Fred and Rose West, which she co-wrote with Stephen Richards.

Caroline continued to have survivor's guilt for the rest of her life. She regretted her decision to not pursue the rape charge against the Wests. She did say, though, that the ordeal gave her a "backbone of steel" and a zest for life she didn't previously have. She said, "You can't keep being the victim. I always used to feel jinxed, like nothing would ever go right for me. Now I have such a zest for life and if I put my mind to something I can do whatever I want."

Caroline died in 2016 after a battle with cancer. Before she died she said she had forgiven Rose West for the horrific abuse.

Marian Partington says she also forgives Rose for murdering her sister, Lucy. She wrote to Rose in prison saying, "I do not feel any hostility towards you, just a deep sadness that all this happened and that your heart could not feel a truth that I wish you could know."

Rose allegedly rejected this forgiveness. Marian received a letter from the prison asking her to "please cease all correspondence, she does not wish to receive any further letters from you". Rose continues to maintain that she is innocent of the murder of Lucy Partington, and of the other nine murders she was charged with.

Marian wrote a book about the loss of her sister and the nature of forgiveness called If You Sit Very Still.

Terry Crick, a former neighbor and friend of Fred, was found dead in his car in January 1996, only a few weeks after he had testified in Rose's trial. Terry had gone to the police in 1970 to report Fred for performing illegal abortions. Terry said Fred had shown him the tools he used to do the procedures, and pictures of women's genitals he had taken after performing the procedure. Fred had wanted Terry to help him find women who needed his services.

Crick's widow, Janet Bates, said, "Terry had been shown disturbing images and went straight to the police but when they didn't do anything he felt responsible."

Terry alleged that Fred was a police informant, and that many officers were actually clients of Rose's. He believed the police had an interest in keeping Fred and Rose on the streets, so they never followed up on his tips, and turned a blind eye to their suspicious behavior.

Janet also says he told her that he had made a full statement to the police after Fred's arrest, but that parts of it were missing when it was read back to him in court at Rose's trial. After the trial he said, "Now Rose has been found guilty I can perhaps give a sigh of relief, but I am sure that there are more bodies."

The stress of the trial, the nagging thought that he was somehow responsible for the murders that happened after his tip was ignored, and his certainty that there were more victims yet to be found led Terry to take his own life by carbon monoxide poisoning.

Conclusion

The effect of Fred and Rosemary West has been far-reaching and devastating. The House of Horrors at 25 Cromwell Street has been totally obliterated, but it will not be as easy to erase the memories of what went on there. The lives of at least twelve people ended, horrifically, and far too soon, at the hands of the Wests. The families of the victims must now attempt to pick up the pieces of their shattered lives and find a way to move on.

Marian Partington has been working toward forgiveness of the Wests since her sister's body was uncovered at 25 Cromwell. She has worked with The Forgiveness Project, an organization that helps people who have suffered through various painful experiences attempt to change their rage and want for revenge into "a quest for restoration and healing."

Her story on The Forgiveness Project website states, "...my work has been about connecting with Rosemary West's humanity and refusing to go down the far easier and more predictable path of demonizing her. I take every opportunity to talk about her as a human being."

People who do bad things are no less human than the rest of us. Demonizing them and wanting them to suffer through the same pain as their victims essentially makes you no better than them. The only way to move forward and find peace with a situation, however horrific, is to find a way to forgive.

Marian concludes her Forgiveness Project story with, "Some people have asked whether I feel I'm betraying Lucy by doing this and I say, 'No, absolutely the opposite: I feel I'm honoring Lucy by lining myself up for forgiveness.'"

Printed in Great Britain
by Amazon